CROWN FINANCIAL MINISTRIES

# BUSINESS BY THE BOOK

## SMALL GROUP STUDY

LARRY BURKETT ◆ HOWARD DAYTON

**LEADER'S GUIDE**

601 Broad St SE
Gainesville GA 30501
1-800-722-1976 / Crown.org

© 2004 by Crown Financial Ministries, Inc.
All rights reserved.

ISBN 1-56427-074-2

Verses identified as (NIV) are taken from the *Holy Bible: New International Version*, copyright 1973, 1978, 1984 by the International Bible Society. Used by permission of Zondervan Bible Publishers.

Verses identified as (AMPLIFIED) are from the *Amplified New Testament*, copyright 1954, 1958, 1987 by The Lockman Foundation. Used by permission.

Verses identified as (TLB) are taken from *The Living Bible*, copyright 1971 by Tyndale House Publishers, Wheaton, Il. Used by permission.

Verses identified as (NJKV) are taken from the *New King James Version*,® copyright ©1982 by Thomas Nelson, Inc. Used by permission. All rights reserved.

All other verses are taken either from the *New American Standard Bible*,® copyright ©1960, 1962, 1963, 1968, 1971, 1972, 1973, 1975, 1977 by The Lockman Foundation, or the *New American Standard Bible*® (updated edition), copyright ©1960, 1962, 1963, 1968, 1971, 1972, 1973, 1975, 1977, 1995 by The Lockman Foundation. Used by permission.

September 2004 Edition

# TABLE OF CONTENTS

| Subject | Pages |
|---|---|
| Course Objectives / Leader's Responsibilities | 4 |
| Information Leaders Need to Know | 5-6 |
| Student Orientation | 7 |
| Prayer Log | 8 |
| Loving the Students | 9 |
| How to Select and Train Leaders | 10 |
| How to Conduct the Study | 11 |
| How to Begin the Study in the Church | 12 |
| Leader's Checklist | 13 |
| Places to Serve | 14 |
| Leader's Weekly Homework Guides | 15-74 |
| Leader's Evaluation and Suggestions, Student Evaluation, Care Log, and Prayer Logs | 75-87 |

## WEB SITE

CROWN has designed a Web site as a resource to provide students with up-to-date financial and business information, helpful articles, additional biblical insights, links to other useful Web sites, and much more.

Visit the Web site at **Crown.org** for a world of information.

## BUSINESS BY THE BOOK

*This small group study is designed to equip business people through learning and applying God's principles for operating a business.*

# Course Objectives/Leader's Responsibilities

## OBJECTIVES OF THE STUDY

1. **Encourage participants to grow in their relationship with Jesus Christ.**

2. **Build close relationships among the participants.**

3. **Help students learn and apply God's principles for operating a business.**

## THE PRIMARY RESPONSIBILITIES OF THE LEADER

1. **Unconditionally love and encourage your students.**
   People are more receptive to spiritual truth when they have been loved. People want to know how much you care before they care how much you know.

2. **Hold your students accountable.**

3. **Be a model of faithfulness.**
   In Luke 6:40 we read, *"Everyone, after he has been fully trained, will be like his teacher."* As a leader, you must be faithful to always arrive early, pray consistently for your students, know the memory verses fluently, and have your homework prepared.

# Information Leaders Need to Know

1. **The Leader's Guide**
   The *Leader's Guide* is divided into three sections:
   - Information the leader needs to know
   - Homework guides
   - Prayer Logs, Care Log, and Student Evaluation

2. ***Business by the Book* conducted identically to CROWN Financial Study**
   The *Business by the Book Small Group Study* has been designed to be conducted and implemented identically to the CROWN's financial study. Once a person has been trained to lead one of the studies, he or she is qualified to lead the other.

3. ***Business by the Book Video***
   Toward the end of class each week, you will play a segment of the *Business by the Book Video*. The video contains eight segments—one for each chapter of the study. For example, at the end of Chapter 4, play Segment 4 of the video. Each segment is about five minutes long.

   The *Business by the Book Video* explains the next chapter's assignment and communicates other important information the students need to know. After viewing the video, answer any questions concerning the assignment. Each small group should have a copy of the video.

4. **Group Size**
   We recommend two leaders in each group.

   The maximum number of students in a group varies, depending on how many students are married couples and how many are individuals. There should be no more than **eight** students. We limit the size of the group because the group dynamic is damaged if the group is too large.

5. **Meeting Time and Location**
   Ideally, the groups should meet for two hours. When this is not possible, you may shorten the time. If the time available is one hour or less, complete half of a chapter each meeting and extend the number of meetings.

   Some groups have required more than eight meetings because of the length of valuable discussion. You may extend the number of meetings at your discretion.

   Convenience for the participants is the key to location. Groups may meet in offices, homes, churches, or any other place that allows for an appropriate level of privacy. Some groups rotate their meetings among the workplaces of the particpants to provide everyone a better sense of each person's work environment.

6. **A Group of Peers**
   We have discovered that *Business by the Book* small groups are most effective when comprised of a group of peers: business owners with business owners, managers with managers, executives with executives. They are generally dealing with similar issues and the discussions are more helpful.

   Some groups are comprised exclusively of couples; some are all men or all women; many are mixed.

## 7. Promoting Financial Products and Services
No one may use their affiliation with *Business by the Book* or CROWN FINANCIAL MINISTRIES to promote or influence the sale of any investments or financial services or professional services.

## 8. Student Evaluation Sheet
The Student Evaluation Sheet is found on page 77 and should be used by the leader to record the performance of the students after each class.

## 9. Scheduling the Study
You may begin a *Business by the Book* small group any time.

## 10. More About *Business by the Book*
The *Business by the Book Small Group Study* is an outreach of CROWN FINANCIAL MINISTRIES. Howard Dayton, cofounder of CROWN, assembled an outstanding group of business people to develop this small group study from the original book and seminar authored by Larry Burkett, the ministry's other cofounder.

## 11. More About CROWN FINANCIAL MINISTRIES
**What is CROWN FINANCIAL MINISTRIES?** CROWN is an interdenominational ministry that has developed a comprehensive program to train people of all ages to apply the Bible's financial principles.

**Why is the ministry named CROWN?** The reason this ministry is named CROWN is to remind us to always honor the Lord and serve people.

- CROWN FINANCIAL MINISTRIES exists to glorify Jesus Christ. He wore a Crown of Thorns when, out of unfathomable love, He died for us (John 19:1-5). Just as the 24 elders in Revelation 4:9-11 cast their crowns before the throne of God, so those serving with CROWN should honor Christ in all that they do.
- CROWN FINANCIAL MINISTRIES exists to serve people. Paul wrote to the Philippians, "*My beloved brothers whom I long to see, my joy and crown*" (Philippians 4:1).

**Financial Information:** CROWN FINANCIAL MINISTRIES is a nonprofit, tax-exempt organization governed by a board of directors, none of whom receive a salary from serving on the CROWN board. Book royalties are the property of the ministry. CROWN is a member of the Evangelical Council for Financial Accountability, whose members must adhere to certain standards, including an annual audit. The ministry is funded primarily by donations, the bulk of which come from graduates of CROWN studies, radio listeners, or churches that are implementing the CROWN program.

# Student Orientation

As the group is being assembled, the leaders should diligently **pray** that the Lord will bring just the right students into the group. Then the leaders should meet with their students as a group at least **two weeks** before the study begins in order to:

### 1. Start to love the students and build relationships.

### 2. Review the requirements.
The requirements are designed to take approximately two hours each week outside of class. If for any reason someone comes to the class unprepared, that person should not be allowed to participate in the discussion. The student requirements:

- Daily homework
- Scripture to memorize each week
- Daily prayer for each participant
- Attend seven of the eight classes

### 3. Describe the other important "ground rules."
- The class opens and closes in prayer.
- Scriptures are memorized in the version used in the *Business by the Book* materials and not in another version of the Bible.
- The classes start and stop on time.
- Group discussions are confidential.
- Students are trained to be future leaders by leading one of the meetings.
- No one will be embarrassed by being required to expose his or her business situation.

### 4. Dispense the materials and collect payment.
One manual is required for each person. Collect payment for the class.

### 5. The Personal Information Sheet.
Ask each student to complete the Personal Information Sheet (found on the last page in the *Business by the Book* manual) and send it to Crown. This is a self-addressed, postage-paid form that does not require an envelope. The Personal Information Sheet may be completed online by visiting Crown.org/Business.

### 6. Assign the Chapter 1 homework.
The assignment is found on page 6 of the manual and should be completed prior to attending Chapter 1. The assignment is to memorize 2 Timothy 3:16-17 and answer the three homework questions. Ask the students to bring their calendars to the first class to schedule the two socials.

# PRAYER LOG

To help the participants develop a more consistent prayer life, we utilize the Prayer Log. During the first meeting, ask each person or couple to provide the information at the top of the Prayer Log: name and personal information.

- One Prayer Log should be filled out for each person or couple.

- End each class by taking prayer requests from each member or couple. The requests need not be limited to financial concerns, and participants may have more than one request. Prior to taking requests, inquire if they have experienced any answers to their prayer requests.

- Ask the participants to complete their own Prayer Logs before coming to class to save time. Each member is required to pray daily for every member in the group during the 8 lessons. Examine the sample Prayer Log below.

### "Pray for one another" (JAMES 5:16).

Name: Don Norman  
Spouse: Janet  
Home phone: 321-2525  
Children (ages): Matthew (12)  
Buisness phone: 542-1378  
Danielle (6)  
E-mail: djnorman@wayout.net  
Home address: 272 Nelsen Ave  
Little Rock AR 72212  

| Chapter | Prayer Request(s) | Answers to Prayer |
|---|---|---|
| 1 | Matthew's cold to get better<br>Don's relationship with boss improve | |
| 2 | Don's relationship with boss improve<br>Janet's neighbor come to know Christ | Matthew is completely well |
| 3 | Pay off business debt | Two major debts have been retired |
| 4 | Pay off business | |
| 5 | | |

# LOVING THE STUDENTS

**1. Love your students outside of class.**

Care Log. The purpose of the Care Log is to ensure that the leaders contact their students each week to encourage and love them. The weekly contacts may be by telephone, mail, e-mail, or in person. The two leaders should alternate each week in their responsibility to contact the students.

The students should not be aware of the Care Log. The leaders should inspect each other's Care Logs weekly to encourage faithfulness.

## CARE LOG

Leaders: **John Cole and Tim Manor**

Beginning Date of Small Group Study: **January 12, 2005**

| CHAPTER | Initials of leader responsible for contact | Student(s) B. Hunt | Student(s) Mr. T Turner Mrs. B Turner | Student(s) J. Morgan | Student(s) G. Jones | Student(s) | Student(s) |
|---|---|---|---|---|---|---|---|
| 1 | JC | Phone 1/13 | Lunch 1/14 | Phone 1/14 | Postcard 1/15 | | |
| 2 | TM | Phone 1/20 | Phone 1/21 | Wrote 1/20 | Saw in person | | |
| 3 | JC | | | | | | |
| 4 | TM | | | | | | |

**Socials.** The leaders should organize two social events for the students. These activities may be for a dessert, a meal, or any other relaxed setting that will encourage the development of relationships. The first social should be scheduled midway through the study. The second social should be held as soon as possible after the study. It is also a good idea to visit the students where they work or live.

**2. Love your students inside of class.**

The leader's attitude should be loving, humble, and caring—not a critical or a know-it-all attitude. We are students-among-students; we all are growing in understanding the unfathomable Word of God.

After a student answers a question, encourage, affirm, and thank that student. If an answer is incorrect, be careful not to discourage the student by responding harshly or negatively. Maintain good eye contact and be attentive because we communicate through our body language.

# How to Select and Train Leaders from Among Your Students

**1. Set the Stage**
In the student orientation, tell your students that you are going to train them to be leaders. Whether they become leaders depends on their desire to lead the study and their faithfulness during the study.

**2. Test your Students**
The most experienced leader should lead Chapters 1 and 2. The co-leader should lead Chapter 3. The students should lead the remaining chapters.

**3. Selection of Leaders**
You should consider only the students who are faithful during the study.

**4. Validation of Leaders**
Any potential leader should be approved by the church leadership, if the study is conducted within a church.

**5. Invitation of Leaders**
After a person has been selected and validated as a leader, invite that person to lead the study. If he or she decides to become a leader, that person needs to be trained.

**6. Training of Leaders**
For your students to be qualified to lead the study, they should do the following.

- Study the *Leader's Guide*.
- Complete a training session during which they view the *Leader's Training Video*. This training session may be conducted by a church or in a citywide event, or it may be a self-study using the video.

# How to Conduct the Study

1. Open with prayer. We recommend that you pray on your knees.
2. Individually recite the Scripture to memorize.
3. Conduct the group discussion. The discussion should proceed as follows.
   - Different group members read the Scriptures for a particular day's homework.
   - Proceed in a circle, asking every person to answer **all** the questions for that day's homework. If the answer to a question is obvious, it is not necessary for more than one person to answer the question.
   - In a couples group, everyone should answer the homework for Day One. Then the men and women should alternate in answering the questions for Days Two through Six.
4. Complete the items listed in the Remaining Agenda in consecutive order.
5. Play the *Business by the Book Video* segment.
6. Share prayer requests and write them in the Prayer Logs.
7. End in prayer.

NOTES

1. **In Chapters 2-8 the homework for Day One always refers to the previous chapter.** This repetition is effective in helping the participants learn.
2. **The homework for Day Six is a Case Study.** It is designed to require more time to complete than the other days' homework.

## SMALL GROUP DYNAMICS

- In Diagram 1 the sole focus is on the leader who does all the talking. The students are passive. This is not how the *Business by the Book Small Group Study* is designed.
- Diagram 2 reflects a group interacting with one another and a leader who guides and facilitates the discussion. The leader must establish an environment in which students have the freedom to express their insights and questions.

DIAGRAM 1
The Wrong Method

DIAGRAM 2
The Correct Method

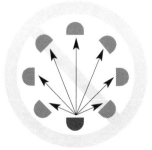

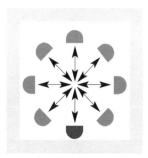

LEADER

LEADER

# How to Begin the Study in the Church

1. **Introduce *Business by the Book Small Group Study* to the pastor/church leadership.**
   Meet with the pastor and appropriate church leadership to explain the study. To successfully implement the study in a church, it is essential to have the active support of the church leadership. The leadership may already be aware of CROWN FINANCIAL MINISTRIES if CROWN's financial program is being conducted in the church.

2. **Select and train the small group leaders.**
   The number of people that will need to be trained is determined by the number of groups the church wants to begin.

3. **Select the students for the initial group or groups.**
   The major objectives of the initial groups are to multiply the number of people qualified to lead.

4. **Choose the initial church coordinator.**
   The church coordinator has the overall responsibility of implementing *Business by the Book Small Group Study* within the church. This position requires a commitment of time and effort and should be a person's primary ministry. The pastor should be involved in the selection process. The church coordinator may be responsible for both *Business by the Book* and CROWN's financial program.

5. **When *Business by the Book* is opened to the church.**
   - Bathe every presentation in prayer, asking the Lord to motivate the students He wants in the study.
   - Communicate the content and benefits of the study, and never use any hard-sell tactics. Describe the requirements and accountability and the need to invest two hours of preparation for each lesson outside of class.
   - Churches have used several methods to present the study: a *Business by the Book Small Group Study* graduate's personal recommendation to a friend, the pastor's recommendation from the pulpit, and an announcement in the church bulletin.

# Leader's Checklist

A four-legged stool symbolizes the four elements a leader must put in place to build a successful small group study.

1. The leader must love the students.
2. The leader must hold the students accountable.
3. The leader must model faithfulness.
4. The leader must conduct the study according to Crown's procedure.

We want to serve you and help you maintain a standard of excellence. In order to assist you, an experienced small group leader may visit your group. After the class has ended and the students have departed, the experienced leader will meet with you to discuss the class and answer any questions. This is the checklist that will be used as a guide.

1. Describe how the leaders **loved** the students.

2. Did the leaders hold the students **accountable** to fulfill their responsibilities?
   - ☐ Scripture Memory
   - ☐ Daily Prayer
   - ☐ Homework

3. Did the leaders **model faithfulness** in the following areas?
   - ☐ Scripture Memory
   - ☐ Daily Prayer
   - ☐ Homework
   - ☐ Care Log / Two Socials Scheduled
   - ☐ Student Evaluation Sheet

4. Did the leaders **conduct the study** according to the Crown agenda?
   - ☐ Start on Time
   - ☐ View Video
   - ☐ Opening Prayer
   - ☐ Prayer Requests
   - ☐ Scripture Memory
   - ☐ Ending Prayer / Stop on Time
   - ☐ Correctly Lead Discussion

# Places to Serve

If you have a desire to help others learn God's ways of operating a business and of handling money, there are four places you can serve with CROWN as illustrated in the baseball diamond.

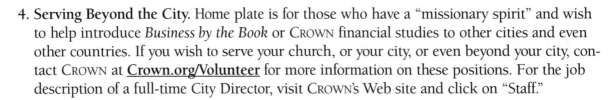

1. **Serving Individuals.** The heroes of the *Business by the Book Small Group Study* are the leaders, because the small group is where life changes take place.

2. **Serving the Church.** If you want to impact your entire church, you may serve as the church coordinator or on the church team.

3. **Serving Your City.** If you have a desire to influence your community, third base is for those who serve as a city director or on the city team.

4. **Serving Beyond the City.** Home plate is for those who have a "missionary spirit" and wish to help introduce *Business by the Book* or CROWN financial studies to other cities and even other countries. If you wish to serve your church, or your city, or even beyond your city, contact CROWN at **Crown.org/Volunteer** for more information on these positions. For the job description of a full-time City Director, visit CROWN's Web site and click on "Staff."

## THE NEXT STEP

1. What I need to do to begin my first group:

   - My leader or co-leader is
   - My potential students are
     (Concentrate on selecting students who have the potential to become future small group leaders. It is also helpful to have someone representing the church leadership participate.)
   - Describe how you will ask the students to participate.
   - Describe how you will schedule the Student Orientation.
   - My goal is to start my first group by this date:

2. What I need to do to help ***Business by the Book*** grow in my church:

   - Meet with my pastor/church leadership to discuss *Business by the Book*.
   - The acting *Business by the Book* church coordinator is
   - Those who will serve on the initial church team are

NOTE: For more information on The Next Step, visit **Crown.org/Business/bbb**.

# Leader's Guide for Chapter 1
# INTRODUCTION

## God's Ways Are Not Our Ways

**OVERVIEW OF CHAPTER 1:** The primary objectives for Chapter 1 are to begin to develop close relationships among the participants and reinforce the study requirements. Leaders should read the Introduction Notes prior to attending class.

**NOTE:** The blank space following each agenda number is for the leader to fill in the scheduled time for each agenda item. For example, if your class begins at 7:00, #1 would read at 7:00, #2 would read at 7:05, #3 would read at 7:10, and so forth. This is designed to assist the leader in monitoring the time so that the class will end punctually.

### AGENDA

1. _____ (5 minutes) **Open in prayer.**

2. _____ (5 minutes) **Each person individually recites from memory 2 Timothy 3:16-17.**

    *"All Scripture is inspired by God and profitable for teaching, for reproof, for correction, for training in righteousness; that the man of God may be adequate, equipped for every good work."*

3. _____ (5 minutes) **Ask the students if they have filled out and mailed (or completed online) the Personal Information Sheet found on the final page of their *Manual*. Review the requirements found on page 4 of the *Manual*.**

4. _____ (70 minutes) **Ask everyone to introduce themselves, beginning with a leader. Ask them to share how they were introduced to Jesus Christ, what they do for a living, and something about their families. To determine how much time each person is allotted, divide the number of people into 70 minutes. The leaders should communicate this time constraint. If a student is too brief, the leader should gently ask additional questions to provide the student with an opportunity to express himself or herself more fully.**

5. _____ (10 minutes) **Begin the homework discussion.**

# HOMEWORK

**Read Isaiah 55:8-9.** *"'My thoughts are not your thoughts, nor are your ways My ways,' declares the Lord. 'For as the heavens are higher than the earth, so are My ways higher than your ways, and My thoughts than your thoughts.'"*

1. Based on this passage, do you think that God's business principles will differ from those used by most people to operate a business? In what ways?

   **Note to Leader:** CROWN's comments, enclosed in brackets, will follow each question. Following CROWN's comments there will be space for the leader's answer.

   [ **Yes. Most people do not believe the Lord plays a part in business, but Scripture reveals that He plays the dominant role.** ]

2. What are the three biggest challenges you are facing in your business?
   - 
   - 
   - 

3. What do want to learn from this study?

## REMAINING AGENDA

1. _____ (5 minutes) **Play the Chapter 1 segment of the *Business by the Book Video*, which reviews what the students are required to do for next week.**

   - Read the Introduction Notes on pages 7-10 in the *Manual*.
   - Complete the Ownership and Purpose Homework on pages 12-16 in the *Manual*.
   - Memorize 1 Chronicles 29:11-12.

2. _____ (5 minutes) **After viewing the Chapter 1 segment of the video, answer any questions the students have about next week's assignment. Remind them to begin memorizing 1 Chronicles 29:11-12 immediately because of its length, and remind them to do the homework daily.**

   - **Review the calendar** to determine if any regularly scheduled classes fall on a holiday. If there are any conflicts, please reschedule at this meeting.
   - **Schedule the two socials**.
   - **Complete the Prayer Logs.** Participants should maintain a separate Prayer Log for each person (or couple) in the group in addition to their own.

3. _____ (10 minutes) **Take prayer requests and note them in the Prayer Log.**

4. _____ (5 minutes) **End in prayer.**

**Reminder for Leaders:** Complete the student evaluations on page 77 in this guide. Decide which leader will be responsible for what week on the Care Log. Be sure to contact each student this week. Encourage students who have not already done so to complete the Personal Information Sheets and send them to Crown Financial Ministries (or complete them online).

## Leader's Guide for Chapter 2
# OWNERSHIP and PURPOSE
## The Lord Is Owner of All

**Reminder:** Complete the students' evaluations. Decide which weeks each leader will take responsibility for the Care Log. Be sure to contact each student this week. Continue to encourage students to complete their Personal Information Sheets online or to mail them to CROWN FINANCIAL MINISTRIES.

**OVERVIEW OF CHAPTER 2:** In many respects this is the most important section because the remainder of the study will build upon understanding God's ownership of all things and His purpose for business. The leaders should read the Ownership and Purpose Notes prior to attending class.

**AGENDA**

1. _____ (5 minutes) **Open in prayer.**

2. _____ (5 minutes) **Each person individually recites from memory 1 Chronicles 29:11-12, TLB.**

   *"Everything in the heavens and earth is yours, O Lord, and this is your kingdom. We adore you as being in control of everything. Riches and honor come from you alone, and you are the Ruler of all mankind; your hand controls power and might, and it is at your discretion that men are made great and given strength."*

3. _____ (80 minutes) **Begin the group discussion.**

> **Reminder:** The discussion for each day's homework should proceed as follows.
> **(1)** Read the Scriptures. Assign one passage of Scripture from that day's homework to each person to read (as far as the verses will go). **(2)** Proceed in a circle, asking each person to answer all the questions for that day's homework. For example, "Bob, how did you answer the questions for day three?" If the answer to a question is obvious, it is not necessary for more than one person to answer the question. If you are running out of time, ask the students for brief responses.

## DAY ONE – REVIEW CHAPTER 1

**Read the Introduction Notes and answer:**

1. What information especially impacted you?

2. How will you apply this in your business life?

## DAY TWO – OWNERSHIP

**Read Psalm 24:1.** *"The earth is the Lord's, and everything in it"* (NIV).

1. What does this passage teach about the ownership of your possessions and business?

   **[ The Lord owns everything in the world including our possessions and business. ]**

2. Prayerfully evaluate your perspective on ownership of your possessions and business. Do you consistently recognize that the Lord owns the business? Give an example of where you have or haven't recognized His ownership.

3. What can you do to more consistently acknowledge His ownership?

## DAY THREE — CONTROL

**Read 1 Chronicles 29:11-12.** *"We adore you as being in control of everything. Riches and honor come from you alone, and you are the Ruler of all mankind; your hand controls power and might, and it is at your discretion that men are made great and given strength"* (TLB).

**And read Psalm 135:6.** *"Whatever the Lord pleases, He does, in heaven and in earth. . . ."*

1. What do these verses say about the Lord's control of your circumstances?

   **[ The Lord is in control of all circumstances. ]**

**Read Isaiah 40:21-24.** *"Do you not know? Have you not heard? . . . He sits enthroned above the circle of the earth, and its people are like grasshoppers. He stretches out the heavens like a canopy, and spreads them out like a tent to live in. He brings princes to naught and reduces the rulers of this world to nothing. No sooner are they planted, no sooner are they sown, no sooner do they take root in the ground, than he blows on them and they wither . . ."* (NIV).

2. What does this passage tell you about the Lord's control of people?

   **[ The Lord has power to control all people, including princes and rulers. ]**

3. Do you currently feel that God is in control of the events in your life? If not, how can you give back control to the Lord?

**Read Genesis 45:5, 8; 50:20.** *"Do not be grieved or angry with yourselves, because you sold me [Joseph] here, for God sent me before you to preserve life.... It was not you who sent me here, but God.... As for you, you meant evil against me, but God meant it for good in order to ... preserve many people alive."*

**And read Romans 8:28.** *"We know that God causes all things to work together for good to those who love God, to those who are called according to His purpose."*

4. Why is it important to realize that God controls and uses even difficult circumstances for good in the life of a godly person?

   **[God works every circumstance for good in the life of those who love Him and are yielded to Him as Lord. Joseph faced difficult circumstances, but God orchestrated those difficulties for ultimate good.]**

5. Share a difficult circumstance you have experienced in business and how the Lord ultimately used it for good in your life.

---

**Leader**—You should have approximately **one hour** of class time remaining. We recommend a three-minute stretch break for your group at this time.

---

## DAY FOUR – PROFESSIONS

1. What are the professions of some of the best-known people of faith in these passages?

   *Abraham (Genesis 13:2, 7)*—**[Shepherd]**

   *Joseph (Genesis 41:39-44)*—**[Prime Minister of Egypt]**

   *Moses (Exodus 3:1)*—**[Shepherd and leader of Israel]**

   *Samuel (1 Samuel 3:20)*—**[Prophet]**

   *David (2 Samuel 5:3)*—**[Shepherd and king]**

2. Why do you think that most of these people of faith were not religious professionals?

[ **God places His people in the marketplace so they can influence people of all walks of life.** ]

3. Why do you think people don't need to be full-time religious professionals (serve as pastors, missionaries, or on the staff of a ministry) before they can have a real impact for Christ? How does this perspective influence the way you view your work?

[ **The Lord will use anyone anywhere who is committed to Him. Those who work in the marketplace can influence people who may never be exposed to a church. It also enables us to model fairness, concern, and honesty that reflect the love of Christ.** ]

**Read Ephesians 2:10.** *"For we are His workmanship, created in Christ Jesus for good works, which God prepared beforehand, that we should walk in them."*

4. What do you think the Lord has created and equipped you to do for a career?

## DAY FIVE – YOUR TRUE BOSS

**Read Colossians 3:23-24.** *"Whatever you do, do your work heartily, as for the Lord rather than for men; knowing that from the Lord you will receive the reward of the inheritance. It is the Lord Christ whom you serve."*

1. For whom do you really work? How will understanding this change your perspective on work?

[ **We work for the Lord. Understanding that we work for the Lord encourages us to do our best and maintain our integrity.** ]

2. What will you do to remind yourself that you are working for Christ?

[ **Frequently review Colossians 3:23-24.** ]

# DAY SIX — CASE STUDY AND APPLICATION

**Note:** You may read the Ownership and Purpose Notes prior to completing Day Six Homework if you wish.

## CASE STUDY

Ted Johnson was a committed Christian who had founded his company to glorify Christ. His company was having a significant impact for Christ on many people. It was also extremely fast growing and successful.

A large corporation approached Ted with an offer to purchase his company. The offering company was reputable and, while not a direct competitor, was very influential in Ted's market niche.

Ted could see the advantages to the sale. The financial resources and reputation of the offering company would provide quicker market penetration and increased profits. More people could be employed. Also, Ted would be released from personal debt that was a source of real stress and receive a sizable amount of cash. He could give much more generously to his church and other ministries. Ted is 55 and has no one who could succeed him to lead the business.

The downside was that the ownership and ultimate decision-making control would be transferred to the purchasing company, with no guarantees that the Christian focus would be continued.

## *Analysis*

1. Define the problem/issue.

2. List the pros and cons of the sale.

3. What are the options and potential consequences?

4. What actions do you think should be taken? Why?

5. How would God be honored and glorified by these actions?

## Application

Based on this case study and what you have learned from the Ownership and Purpose lesson, answer the following questions.

1. What insight have you gained concerning your business?

2. What changes might you need to make in the operation of your business?

3. What results would you hope to see?

4. Complete the Quit Claim Deed on the following page, transferring ownership of your business to the Lord.

---

**REMAINING AGENDA**

1. _____ (10 minutes) **Play the Chapter 2 segment of the *Business by the Book Video*,** which reviews what the students are required to do for next week. Answer any questions they may have.

    - Read the Ownership and Purpose Notes on pages 18-24 in the *Manual*.
    - Complete the Leadership Homework on pages 28-33 in the *Manual*.
    - Memorize Philippians 2:3.

2. _____ (10 minutes) **Note requests and answers to prayer in the Prayer Log.**
3. _____ (5 minutes) **End in prayer.**

**Reminder:** Remember to be vulnerable regarding your own business challenges. Contact each student this week and record the communication in the Care Log. Please review the mechanics of how to lead the group discussion on page 11 to confirm that you are conducting the discussion correctly.

# Quit Claim Deed

**This Quit Claim Deed**, Made the _____ day of _____

From: _____

To:  The Lord

I (we) hereby transfer to the Lord the ownership of the following possessions:

Witnesses who hold me (us) accountable
in the recognition of the Lord's ownership:

_____

_____

_____

Stewards of the possessions above:

_____

_____

This instrument is not a binding legal document and cannot be used to transfer property.

# Leader's Guide for Chapter 3
# LEADERSHIP
## God's Leader Is a Servant

**OVERVIEW OF CHAPTER 3:** The success of any business can be traced back to leadership. This chapter challenges us to follow the Lord's example of servant-leadership. The leader should read the Leadership Notes prior to attending class.

### AGENDA:

1. _____ (5 minutes) **Open in prayer.**

2. _____ (5 minutes) **Each person individually recites from memory Philippians 2:3.**

    *"Do nothing from selfishness or empty conceit, but with humility of mind let each of you regard one another as more important than himself."*

4. _____ (85 minutes) **Begin the group discussion.**

> **Reminder:** Do not read the notes in class.

## DAY ONE – REVIEW CHAPTER 2 NOTES

**Read the Ownership and Purpose Notes and answer.**

1. What in the Notes was particularly helpful or challenging?

2. How will you apply what you learned to your personal and business life?

## DAY TWO – LEADERSHIP

**Read Mark 10:42-44.** *"Jesus . . . said, 'You know that those who are regarded as rulers of the Gentiles lord it over them, and their high officials exercise authority over them. Not so with you. Instead, whoever wants to become great among you must be your servant, and whoever wants to be first must be slave of all"* (NIV).

1. What does Jesus say about leadership?

   **[ Godly leaders are servants. ]**

2. Give some examples of His leadership style.

   **[ He was sensitive to the needs of people around him: He fed them, healed them, taught them, modeled truth for them, and prayed for them. Jesus forgave the failures of His followers and entrusted them with great responsibility. He loved and served others. ]**

3. How is this contrary to the way most business leaders operate?

   **[ It is totally contrary because most business leaders are primarily concerned for their own welfare and reputation. ]**

4. How would others describe your leadership strengths and weaknesses?

**Read Philippians 2:3-4.** *"Do nothing out of selfish ambition or vain conceit, but in humility consider others better than yourselves. Each of you should look not only to your own interests, but also to the interests of others"* (NIV).

5. What does this passage communicate concerning caring for others?

   [ **We need to value others as more important than ourselves. We need to consciously train ourselves to be alert to their needs and to serve them.** ]

6. List three examples of how you care for your staff at work.

## DAY THREE – BUSINESS RELATIONSHIPS

**Read Ephesians 6:5-8.** *"Slaves [employees], obey your earthly masters [employers] with respect and fear, and with sincerity of heart, just as you would obey Christ. Obey them not only to win their favor when their eye is on you, but like slaves of Christ, doing the will of God from your heart. Serve wholeheartedly, as if you were serving the Lord, not men, because you know that the Lord will reward everyone for whatever good he does"* (NIV).

1. What does this passage tell us about how you should relate to your superiors? List any areas in which you need to improve.

   [ **We should serve superiors sincerely, wholeheartedly, and to the best of our ability whether in public or private. We should work for them as we would for the Lord.** ]

**Read Ephesians 6:9.** *"And masters [employers], treat your slaves [employees] in the same way. Do not threaten them, since you know that he who is both their Master and yours is in heaven, and there is no favoritism with him"* (NIV).

2. What does this verse say about how we should relate to those under our authority?

   [ **We should treat them with respect. We should not threaten them, knowing that God is the Master over us all. His impartiality will not overlook injustice in the authority we exercise.** ]

**Read Psalms 78:72.** *"So he [King David]* **shepherded them** *[his subordinates] according to the integrity of his heart, and guided them with his skillful hands."*

3. What are some practical ways that you can be a shepherd-leader at work?

> **Leader—** You should have approximately **one hour** of class time remaining. We recommend a three-minute stretch break for your group at this time.

## DAY FOUR – COUNSEL

**Read Proverbs 12:15.** *"The way of a fool is right in his own eyes, but a wise man is he who listens to counsel."*

**And read Proverbs 15:22.** *"Without consultation, plans are frustrated, but with many counselors they succeed."*

1. What are some benefits of seeking counsel?

> *Proverbs 12:15* — [ **The person who listens to counsel gains wisdom.** ]

> *Proverbs 15:22* — [ **Plans are successful with many counselors.** ]

2. What hinders you from seeking counsel?

**Read Psalm 16:7.** *"I will praise the Lord, who counsels me; even at night my heart instructs me"* (NIV).

**And read Psalm 32:8.** *"I [the Lord] will instruct you and teach you in the way you should go; I will counsel you and watch over you"* (NIV).

3. Does the Lord actively counsel His children? How?

   **[ Yes, the Lord counsels us as we read His Word and pray. ]**

4. Have you ever suffered for not seeking the Lord's counsel? If so, describe what happened.

## DAY FIVE — COUNSEL

**Read Psalm 119:105.** *"Your word is a lamp to my feet, and a light for my path"* (NIV).

**And read Hebrews 4:12.** *"For the Word of God is living and active. Sharper than any double-edged sword. . . . It judges the thoughts and attitudes of the heart"* (NIV).

1. Should the Bible also serve as your counselor? Why?

   **[ Yes, we must seek the counsel of the Word of God because it gives us direction for our lives. ]**

2. Do you consistently read and study the Bible? If not, why?

**Read Proverbs 11:14.** *"Where there is no guidance, the people fall. But in abundance of counselors there is victory."*

**And read Ecclesiastes 4:9-10. 12.** *"Two are better than one because they have a good return for their labor. For if either of them falls, the one will lift up his companion. But woe to the one who falls when there is not another to lift him. . . . If one can overpower him who is alone, two can resist him. A cord of three strands is not quickly torn apart."*

3. What do these verses say to you?

> *Proverbs 11:14*—[ **Without guidance, people fall; but counsel will bring victory.** ]

> *Ecclesiastes 4:9-10, 12*—[ **Two or three people working together will accomplish more than people working alone.** ]

4. How do you propose to apply this principle in your personal and business life?

5. In your opinion, who should be the number-one counselor of a husband? Of a wife? Why?

   [ **A husband and wife should be each other's primary counselor. Decisions made by either of them have an impact on the other.** ]

**Read Psalm 1:1.** *"How blessed is the man who does not walk in the counsel of the wicked, nor stand in the path of sinners, nor sit in the seat of scoffers."*

6. Whom should you avoid as a counselor? Why?

   [ **Avoid the the wicked as counselors, because any insight they may have is worldly and not based on the truth of God's Word.** ]

# DAY SIX – CASE STUDY AND PRACTICAL APPLICATION

**Note:** You may choose to read the Leadership Notes prior to completing this Day Six Homework.

## CASE STUDY

Harvey Peterson was the CEO of a small manufacturing operation who had never taken the time to document the core values of the business. He hired a plant manager. During the interview, the applicant commented that he was not a Christian but would have no problem working in a Christian environment.

The new manager freed up Harvey's time to pursue marketing and sales planning, and as a result, sales and profits increased substantially. The manager and his wife decided to use one of his first bonus checks to make the down payment on a home.

However, the new manager was lax about safety, break time limits, and plant cleanliness. Attempts to minister to the plant staff were damaged by the manager's rude and verbally abusive manner. Some key employees quit because of it. Harvey counseled the manager, but the manager made no changes.

Harvey was in doubt. If he discharged the manager, it would financially hurt the manager's family. But continuing to have him on staff would potentially damage the company's witness to the other employees.

## *Analysis*

1. Define the problem/issue.

2. Identify the people involved.

3. What decisions must be made and what are the potential consequences?

4. What actions do you think should be taken? Why?

5. How would God be honored and glorified by these actions?

*Application*
Based on this case study and what you have learned from the Leadership lesson, answer the following questions.

1. What principles will you apply to your business?

2. What changes might you need to make in the operation of your business?

3. What results would you hope to see?

**PRACTICAL APPLICATION**
Identify the *core values* of your business or department and describe how you are going to help everyone learn and apply them.

---

**REMAINING AGENDA**

1. _____ (10 minutes) **Play the Chapter 3 segment of the *Business by the Book Video*.**
   - Read the Leadership Notes on pages 34-42 in the *Manual*.
   - Complete the Finance Homework on pages 46-52 in the *Manual*.
   - Memorize Proverbs 22:7.

2. _____ (10 minutes) **Note requests and answers to prayer in the Prayer Logs.**

3. _____ (5 minutes) **End in prayer.**

**Reminder:** In order to recognize God's ownership more consistently, encourage the participants to continue meditating on *1 Chronicles 29:11-12*. Contact each student this week and note this in the Care Log. Remind the students to visit Crown's Web site at **Crown.org/Business** for more helpful resources.

# Leader's Guide for Chapter 4
# FINANCE
## Get Out of Debt

**OVERVIEW OF CHAPTER 4:** Almost every decision in business has a financial impact. Debt, lending, receivables, and business giving are all important issues. The leader should read the Finance Notes prior to attending class.

**AGENDA**

1. _____ (5 minutes) **Open in prayer.**

2. _____ (5 minutes) **Each person individually recites from memory Proverbs 22:7, TLB.**
   *"Just as the rich rule the poor, so the borrower is servant to the lender."*

3. _____ (80 minutes) **Begin the group discussion.**

## DAY ONE – REVIEW CHAPTER 3 NOTES

**Read the Leadership Notes and answer.**

1. What in the Notes was particularly helpful or challenging?

2. How will you apply what you learned to your personal and business life?

## DAY TWO – DEBTS

**Read Romans 13:8.** *"Keep out of debt and owe no man anything"* (AMPLIFIED).

**And read Proverbs 22:7.** *"Just as the rich rule the poor, so the borrower is servant to the lender"* (TLB).

1. Is debt encouraged in Scripture? Why?

   *Romans 13:8*—[ **No, we are encouraged to stay out of debt.** ]

   *Proverbs 22:7*—[ **Debt puts us in bondage to the lender.** ]

2. How does this apply to you personally and to your business?

3. If you are in debt, do you have a strategy to eliminate it? If you have a plan, please describe it.

**Read Deuteronomy 28:1-2, 12.** *"If you diligently obey the Lord your God, being careful to do all His commandments which I command you today, the Lord your God will set you high above all the nations of the earth. All these blessings will come upon you and overtake you, if you obey the Lord your God. . . . And you shall lend to many nations, but you shall not borrow."*

**And read Deuteronomy 28:15, 43-44.** *"If you do not obey the Lord your God, to observe to do all His commandments and His statutes with which I charge you today, that all these curses will come upon you. . . . The alien who is among you shall rise above you higher and higher, but you will go down lower and lower. He shall lend to you, but you will not lend to him."*

4. According to these passages, how was debt viewed in the Old Testament?

   **[ Debt was considered a curse. Being out of debt (being a lender) was a blessing. ]**

5. What was the cause of someone getting into debt (becoming a borrower) or getting out of debt (becoming a lender)?

   **[ Disobedience led to debt. Obedience led to getting out of debt (being a lender). ]**

## DAY THREE – DEBT REPAYMENT AND LAWSUITS

**Read Psalm 37:21.** *"The wicked borrows and does not pay back, but the righteous is gracious and gives."*

**And Read Proverbs 3:27-28.** *"Do not withhold good from those to whom it is due, when it is in your power to do it. Do not say to your neighbor, 'Go, and come back, and tomorrow I will give it,' when you have it with you."*

1. What do these verses say about debt repayment?

   *Psalm 37:21*—**[ A person who borrows but does not repay is called "wicked." ]**

   *Proverbs 3:27-28*—**[ Pay debts promptly if you have the resources. Delaying repayment to use other people's money as long as possible is not biblical. ]**

2. How will you implement this principle in your business?

**Read 1 Corinthians 6:1-7.** *"If any of you has a dispute with another, dare he take it before the ungodly for judgment instead of before the saints? Do you not know that the saints will judge the world? And if you are to judge the world, are you not competent to judge trivial cases? Do you not know that we will judge angels? How much more the things of this life! Therefore, if you have disputes about such matters, appoint as judges even men of little account in the church! I say this to shame you. Is it possible that there is nobody among you wise enough to judge a dispute between believers? But instead, one brother goes to law against another—and this in front of unbelievers! The very fact that you have lawsuits among you means you have been completely defeated already. Why not rather be wronged? Why not rather be cheated?"* (NIV).

3. When is it acceptable to take another believer to court? Why?

> **[ It is unacceptable to take a fellow believer to court. Instead, believers should settle their disputes with each other before wise people within the church. ]**

**Read Matthew 18:15-17.** *"If your brother sins, go and show him his fault in private; if he listens to you, you have won your brother. But if he does not listen to you, take one or two more with you, so that by the mouth of two or three witnesses every fact may be confirmed. If he refuses to listen to them, tell it to the church; and if he refuses to listen even to the church, let him be to you as a Gentile and a tax collector."*

4. Describe God's procedure for Christians resolving disputes among themselves.

> **[ Step One: Go to the offending person and seek resolution in private. If that fails, Step Two is to take one or two people to help establish the facts and resolve the issue. If that fails, Step Three is to go before the church to resolve the issue. If that fails, Step Four is to treat the offender as an unbeliever. ]**

5. Do you have a policy on how to collect past-due receivables? If so, describe it.

> **Leader** — You should have approximately **one hour** of class time remaining. We recommend a three-minute stretch break for your group at this time.

## DAY FOUR – GIVING

**Read 1 Corinthians 13:3.** *"If I give all my possessions to feed the poor . . . but do not have love, it profits me nothing."*

**And read 2 Corinthians 9:7.** *"Each one must do just as he has purposed in his heart, not grudgingly or under compulsion, for God loves a cheerful giver.."*

1. What do these passages say about the importance of the proper attitude in giving?

    *1 Corinthians 13:3*—[**Giving that is not motivated by love is of no value to the giver.**]

    *2 Corinthians 9:7*—[**God is more concerned about our attitude in giving than just the amount we give. He desires us to give cheerfully, not grudgingly.**]

2. How do you think can a person develop the proper attitude in giving?

    [**The proper attitude is the key issue in the area of giving. The only way to give consistently out of a heart of love is to consciously give each gift to Jesus Christ Himself as an act of worship.**]

3. After prayerfully evaluating your attitude in giving, how would you describe it?

**Read Acts 20:35.** *"Remember the words of the Lord Jesus, that He Himself said, 'It is more blessed to give than to receive.'"*

4. How does this principle from God's economy differ from the way most people view giving?

    [**Most people assume the opposite: that they experience more benefits from receiving than giving.**]

**Read Proverbs 11:24-25.** *"There is one who scatters, and yet increases all the more, and there is one who withholds what is justly due, and yet it results only in want. The generous man will be prosperous, and he who waters will himself be watered."*

**And read Luke 12:34.** *"For where your treasure is, there your heart will be also."*

5. List the benefits for the giver that are found in these passages:

    *Proverbs 11:24-25*—[ **There is a material increase—in the Lord's time and way—to the giver.** ]

    *Luke 12:34*—[ **The heart of the giver is drawn to Christ as treasures are given to Him.** ]

## DAY FIVE – AMOUNT TO GIVE

**Read Malachi 3:8-11.** *"Will a man rob God? Yet you are robbing Me! But you say, 'How have we robbed You?' In tithes and offerings. You are cursed with a curse, for you are robbing Me, the whole nation of you! Bring the whole tithe into the storehouse, so that there may be food in My house, and test Me now in this,' says the Lord of hosts, 'if I will not open for you the windows of heaven and pour out for you a blessing until it overflows. Then I will rebuke the devourer for you, so that it will not destroy the fruits of the ground; nor will your vine in the field cast its grapes,' says the Lord of hosts."*

1. Was the tithe (giving 10 percent) required under Old Testament Law? How do you think it applies today?

   [ **Yes. God considered it robbery when His people failed to tithe.** ]

**Read 2 Corinthians 8:1-5.** *"Brothers, we want you to know about the grace that God has given the Macedonian churches. Out of the most severe trial, their overflowing joy and their extreme poverty welled up in rich generosity. For I testify that they gave as much as they were able, and even beyond their ability. Entirely on their own, they urgently pleaded with us for the privilege of sharing in this service to the saints. And they did not do as we expected, but they gave themselves first to the Lord and then to us in keeping with God's will"* (NIV).

2. Identify principles from this passage that should influence how much you give.

   [ **1. They first gave themselves to the Lord, asking Him to direct their giving. In the same way, we need to submit ourselves to the Lord when determining how much to give.** ]

   [ **2. They were so yielded to the Lord that despite difficult circumstances they begged to give.** ]

   [ **3. They experienced tremendous joy as a result of their sacrificial giving.** ]

3. If you are in a position to make this decision, prayerfully seek the Lord's guidance to determine how much your business should give. If you are married, ask your spouse to join you in this determination. You will not be asked to disclose the amount.

## DAY SIX – CASE STUDY AND PRACTICAL APPLICATION

**Note:** You may choose to read the Finance Notes prior to completing Day Six Homework.

**CASE STUDY**

Sarah was a very visible Christian in the community. Her construction supply business had grown substantially for several years during prosperous times in the local economy. Credit was readily available, and Sarah had borrowed extensively, leveraged her receivables, and cosigned the notes to expand the business. She was required to provide monthly financial statements as a condition of the financing.

The economy slowed, sales were off, and there were rumors that her lender was preparing to discontinue lending to the construction industry. The current month's financial statement reflected a moderate loss, and Sarah was afraid that her credit line would be closed if she didn't continue to show a profit.

She had received a large order that was to be shipped next month. If it were included in the current financials, the company would show a profit for the month. Sarah was confident that the rest of next month's sales would be sufficient to make up the difference.

### *Analysis*

1. Define the problem/issue.

2. Identify the people involved.

3. Identify special circumstances and potential consequences.

4. What actions do you think should be taken? Why?

5. How would God be honored and glorified by these actions?

## Application
Based on this case study and what you have learned from the Finance lesson, answer the following questions.

1. What insight have you gained concerning your business?

2. What changes might you need to make in the operation of your business?

3. What results would you hope to see?

## PRACTICAL APPLICATION
Complete the Debt List on the following page, and describe below your plan for reducing or eliminating your business debt.

---

**REMAINING AGENDA**

1. _____ (10 minutes) **Play the Chapter 4 segment of the *Business by the Book Video*. Answer any questions the participants may have.**
   - Read the Finance Notes on pages 54-65 in the *Manual*.
   - Complete the Human Resources Homework on pages 68-73 in the *Manual*.
   - Memorize Luke 16:10.

2. _____ (10 minutes) **Note requests and answers to prayer in the Prayer Logs.**

3. _____ (5 minutes) **End in prayer.**

**Reminder:** Remember to complete the Student Evaluations.

# Debt List

Date: _____

| Creditor | Describe What Was Purchased | Monthly Payments | Balance Due | Scheduled Pay Off Date | Interest Rate | Payments Past Due |
|---|---|---|---|---|---|---|
|  |  |  |  |  |  |  |
|  |  |  |  |  |  |  |
|  |  |  |  |  |  |  |
|  |  |  |  |  |  |  |
|  |  |  |  |  |  |  |
|  |  |  |  |  |  |  |
|  |  |  |  |  |  |  |
|  |  |  |  |  |  |  |
|  |  |  |  |  |  |  |
|  |  |  |  |  |  |  |
|  |  |  |  |  |  |  |
|  |  |  |  |  |  |  |
|  |  |  |  |  |  |  |
|  |  |  |  |  |  |  |
| **Totals** |  |  |  |  |  |  |

### Auto Loans

|  |  |  |  |  |  |  |
|---|---|---|---|---|---|---|
|  |  |  |  |  |  |  |
|  |  |  |  |  |  |  |
|  |  |  |  |  |  |  |
| **Total Auto Loans** |  |  |  |  |  |  |

### Home Mortgages

|  |  |  |  |  |  |  |
|---|---|---|---|---|---|---|
|  |  |  |  |  |  |  |
|  |  |  |  |  |  |  |
|  |  |  |  |  |  |  |
| **Total Home Mortgages** |  |  |  |  |  |  |

### Business/Investment Debt

|  |  |  |  |  |  |  |
|---|---|---|---|---|---|---|
|  |  |  |  |  |  |  |
|  |  |  |  |  |  |  |
|  |  |  |  |  |  |  |
|  |  |  |  |  |  |  |
|  |  |  |  |  |  |  |
|  |  |  |  |  |  |  |
| **Total Business/Investment Debt** |  |  |  |  |  |  |

# Leader's Guide for Chapter 5
# HUMAN RESOURCES

**OVERVIEW OF CHAPTER 5:** People are the most valuable asset of any business. God places a high value on each individual, and so should we. Read the Human Resources Notes prior to attending class.

**AGENDA:**

1. _____ (5 minutes) **Open in prayer.**

2. _____ (5 minutes) **Each person individually recites from memory:**

   *"He who is faithful in a very little thing is faithful also in much"* (Luke 16:10).

3. _____ (85 minutes) **Begin the group discussion.**

## DAY ONE – REVIEW CHAPTER 4

**Read the Finance Notes and answer.**

1. What in the Notes was particularly helpful or challenging?

2. How will you apply what you learned to your personal and business life?

Note: Even if you don't have employees in your business, the principles you will learn in this chapter are applicable to other areas (e.g., church, professional associations) in which you serve in a leadership role.

## DAY TWO – HIRING

**Read Luke 6:12-13.** *"Jesus went out to a mountainside to pray, and spent the night praying to God. When morning came, he called his disciples to him and chose twelve of them, whom he also designated apostles"* (NIV).

1. How much time did Jesus Christ invest praying about the selection of the 12 apostles?

    **[ Jesus spent a significant amount of time praying for direction on the selection of His key people. ]**

2. How does this apply to you when you are seeking to hire employees? Do you consistently commit to pray?

    **[ We should seek God's guidance in all important decisions, especially key personnel decisions. ]**

3. Discuss the process you use when hiring.

4. Do you think you need to improve any areas of hiring? If so, what?

5. Do you hire only Christians in your business? Why or why not?

## DAY THREE – PROMOTION

**Read Genesis 39:5.** *"It came about that from the time he* [Joseph's Egyptian boss] *made him overseer in his house, and over all that he owned, the Lord blessed the Egyptian's house on account of Joseph."*

**And read Matthew 25:23.** *"His master replied, 'Well done, good and faithful servant! You have been faithful with a few things; I will put you in charge of many things. Come and share your master's happiness!'"* (NIV).

1. What are some of the things we should look for when considering a person for promotion?

    *Genesis 39:5*— [**Is there evidence of God's blessing on this person's life? Does this person have an attitude that would be appropriate for God to bless?**]

    *Matthew 25:23*— [**Has the person been faithful in the discharge of previous responsibilities?**]

**Read 1 Timothy 3:2-3.** *"Now the overseer must be above reproach, the husband of but one wife, temperate, self-controlled, respectable, hospitable, able to teach, not given to drunkenness, not violent but gentle, not quarrelsome, not a lover of money"* (NIV),

2. What character qualities from this passage do you look for when promoting people to leadership positions?

3. What are the most valuable insights you have learned from experience about promoting people?

4. Describe any lessons you have learned the hard way from unsuccessful promotions.

> **Leader**—You should have approximately **one hour** of class time remaining. We recommend a three-minute stretch break for your group at this time.

## DAY FOUR – ACCOUNTABILITY

**Read Matthew 25:19.** *"Now after a long time the master of those slaves came and settled accounts with them."*

1. According to this passage, do you think the Lord approves of holding people accountable to be faithful in the handling of responsibilities?

    **[ Just as the master in the parable held the servants accountable and the Lord holds us accountable, we should hold people accountable to be faithful in their work. ]**

2. How do you apply the principle of accountability to your staff?

**Read Hebrews 12:10-11.** *"He [the Lord] disciplines us for our good, that we might share His holiness. All discipline for the moment seems not to be joyful, but sorrowful; yet to those who have been trained by it, afterwards it yields the peaceful fruit of righteousness."*

3. What does this passage say about discipline?

    **[ The Lord's discipline is for our good. Although we do not enjoy it at the moment, we benefit from it. ]**

**Read 1 Corinthians 15:33.** *"Do not be deceived: 'Bad company corrupts good morals.'"*

4. According to this verse, how will a dishonest or rebellious employee influence other employees?

    **[ A dishonest or rebellious employee will be a corrupting influence on others. ]**

5. Describe the process you use to dismiss an employee.

# DAY FIVE – PAY

**Read Malachi 3:5.** *"Then I [the Lord] will draw near to you for judgment; and I will be a swift witness . . . against who oppress the wage earner in his wages."*

**And read James 5:4.** *"The pay of the laborers who mowed your fields, and which has been withheld by you, cries out against you."*

1. What do these verses say to you about paying employees fairly?

   [**God is aware of any unfairness we allow and will discipline us for mistreatment of our workers.**]

2. Do you feel you pay adequate wages? Why or why not?

**Read Colossians 4:1.** *"Masters [employers], grant to your slaves [employees] justice and fairness, knowing that you too have a Master in heaven."*

3. How can an employer apply this principle?

   [**Always treat your employees fairly.**]

**Read 1 Corinthians 12:24-26.** *"God has combined the members of the body and has given greater honor to the parts that lacked it, so that there should be no division in the body, but that its parts should have equal concern for each other. If one part suffers, every part suffers with it; if one part honored, every part rejoices with it"* (NIV).

4. How can you apply the principles of honor and recognition within the Body of Christ to a business environment?

   [**Promote the importance of the team and the value of all members in light of their unique and necessary contributions to the team. Look for opportunities to celebrate the achievements and faithfulness of those who might normally be overlooked. Foster a culture of care so that team members cheer for each other in times of victory and help share the load in times of difficulty.**]

5. What are some of the practical approaches you have used to honor faithful employees?

# DAY SIX – CASE STUDY AND PRACTICAL APPLICATION

**Note:** You may choose to read the Human Resources Notes prior to completing Day Six Homework.

## CASE STUDY

Chuck has been striving to make his company a platform for ministry. When it came time to replace the controller, he looked for a Christian. He found and hired a highly qualified one.

When his accounting clerk learned of the new controller, she demanded a 50 percent raise and a major promotion. She had been with the company for 11 years but was not qualified for the position she wanted. She was informed that it would not be possible to meet her demands. She resigned without notice rather than orient her new boss to the computerized accounting and payroll systems.

Five months later, Chuck was notified that the woman had filed an EEOC complaint against his company. She charged religious and gender discrimination because she had not been promoted to fill the controller's position.

Chuck had not considered the woman a candidate because she did not have the necessary professional qualifications. He obtained the best Christian labor attorney in the city to prepare his defense. After months of discussion, depositions, and briefs, the attorney assured Chuck that they had a solid case.

However, the attorney also told Chuck that the hearing process was unpredictable, and that an adverse ruling would be expensive. In the highly politicized climate in their state, anything could happen. He suggested that Chuck begin praying about the possibility of an out-of-court settlement. Should Chuck settle and put a limit on his liability or should he continue to defend himself to the end?

## *Analysis*

1. Define the problem/issue.

2. Identity the people involved.

3. Identify special circumstances and potential consequences.

4. What actions do you think should be taken? Why?

5. How would God be honored and glorified by these actions?

## *Application*

Based on this case study and what you have learned from the Human Resources lesson, answer the following questions.

1. What insight have you gained concerning your business?

2. What changes might you need to make in the operation of your business?

3. What results would you hope to see?

**PRACTICAL APPLICATION**
Describe your hiring process and policies. What changes do you feel are necessary and how will you implement them?

**REMAINING AGENDA**

1. _____(10 minutes) **Play the Chapter 5 segment of the *Business By The Book Video*. Answer any of the participants' questions.**

   - Read the Human Resources Notes on pages 74-90 in the *Manual*.
   - Complete the Organization Homework on 94-99 in the *Manual*.
   - Memorize 2 Corinthians 6:14.

2. **Ask students to recommend and/or contact people who might be future students. Forward any recommendations to the *Business By The Book* or CROWN FINANCIAL MINISTRIES church or city leader.**

3. _____(10 minutes) **Note requests and answers to prayers in the Prayer Log.**

4. _____(5 minutes) **End in prayer.**

# Leader's Guide for Chapter 6
# ORGANIZATION

**OVERVIEW OF CHAPTER 6:** The organizational structure of a business has a lot to do with its success. This chapter may not be currently applicable to everyone in the class, but the principles are important for everyone to understand. Read the Organization Notes prior to attending class.

**AGENDA:**

1._____ (5 minutes) **Open in prayer.**

2._____ (5 minutes) **Each individual recites from memory:**

> *"Do not be bound together with unbelievers; for what partnership have righteousness and lawlessness, or what fellowship has light with darkness?"* (2 Corinthians 6:14)

3._____ (85 minutes) **Begin the group discussion.**

## DAY ONE – REVIEW CHAPTER 5

**Read the Human Resources Notes and answer.**

1. What in the Notes was particularly helpful or challenging?

2. How will you apply what you learned to your personal and business life?

## DAY TWO – CORE VALUES AND TEAMWORK

1. Have you documented in writing the values (core values) for your business that you will not compromise under any circumstances? If so, list the most important core values.

2. Do you have a strategy to use teamwork effectively in your business? (Even if you operate a one-person business, you will need to work with vendors, referral sources, etc.) If so, please describe it.

## DAY THREE – BUSINESS PARTNERSHIPS

1. What are the most common reasons for creating a business partnership?

   [ **The most common reasons for starting a partnership are to raise capital and to bring expertise or labor to a business.** ]

**Read 2 Corinthians 6:14-15.** *"Do not be bound together with unbelievers; for what partnership have righteousness and lawlessness, or what fellowship has light with darkness? Or what harmony has Christ with Belial, or what has a believer in common with an unbeliever?"*

2. How can you apply the principle in this passage to business partnerships?

   [ **The Lord discourages a Christian from entering into a partnership with a person who does not know Christ.** ]

3. Have you been in a business partnership? If so, what has your experience been?

> **Leader**—You should have approximately **one hour** of class time remaining. We recommend a three-minute stretch break for your group at this time.

## DAY FOUR – BUSINESS PARTNERSHIPS AND PRIVATELY HELD CORPORATIONS

1. If you consider forming a partnership or privately held corporation with a person who knows Christ, what issues do you think you need to agree upon before entering into the partnership or corporation?

2. If you are married, describe how you would involve your spouse in this decision.

3. What personal character qualities would a potential partner or closely held stockholder need to have?

4. How should you document your agreement with a potential partner or stockholder?

5. Describe your agreement if a partner or stockholder wishes to leave the partnership or corporation. Do you have a buy-sell agreement?

**Read Ephesians 6:2-3.** *"Honor your father and mother (which is the first commandment with a promise), so that it may be well with you, and that you may live long on the earth."*

6. What adjustments would you make in your Day Three answers if you were dealing with family members?

7. If you are in an existing partnership with your parents (and they do not yet know the Lord), how do you seek to honor them in the partnership?

   **[If the parents desire for you to remain in the partnership, do so unless you would be required to compromise your integrity or receive the Lord's clear direction to do something else.]**

## DAY FIVE – FORM OF BUSINESS

**Read Ephesians 6:5-6.** *"Slaves* [employees], *obey your earthly masters* [employers] *with respect and fear, and with sincerity of heart, just as you would obey Christ"* (NIV).

1. Do you think that an employer-employee relationship with a non-Christian violates the principle of not being bound together? Why or why not?

   **[No. Since the employer is clearly the authority, it is not a partnership relationship in which both can make decisions that will legally bind the other.]**

2. Describe the form of your business (sole proprietorship, partnership, or corporation).

3. Describe the personal benefits as well as the disadvantages you have experienced using this form of ownership.

## DAY SIX – CASE STUDY

**NOTE:** You may choose to read the Organization Notes prior to completing Day Six Homework.

**CASE STUDY**

Luke Allison, a committed Christian, owned a real estate company in a community with a changing business climate. He served a bedroom community of 120,000 people, many of whom worked in the neighboring city. The home sales market was very slow.

Maintaining an independent firm was basic to his approach to business. However, he was losing market share to the large national realtors who had moved into his town. These national firms not only were attracting buyers but also his salespeople.

A respected long-term realtor in the community suggested a business venture to Luke. They would merge the two businesses and together attract more experienced salespeople who did not prefer a large national company. This would stabilize their business and provide them the opportunity to expand into the major metropolitan market as well.

### Analysis

1. Define the problem/issue.

2. Identity the people involved.

3. Identify special circumstances and potential consequences.

4. What actions do you think should be taken? Why?

5. How would God be honored and glorified by these actions?

*Application*
Based on this case study and what you have learned from the Organization lesson, please answer the following questions.

1. What insight have you gained concerning your business?

2. What changes might you need to make in the operation of your business?

3. What results would you hope to see?

**PRACTICAL APPLICATION**
Analyze the ownership of your existing business or the business you are contemplating. Describe what changes, if any, you need to make.

**REMAINING AGENDA**

1. _____ (10 minutes) **Play the Chapter 6 segment of the *Business By The Book Video*. Answer any questions.**

   - Read the Organization Notes on pages 100-110 in the *Manual*.
   - Complete the Marketing Homework on pages 112-117 in the *Manual*.
   - Memorize Leviticus 19:11.

2. _____ (10 minutes) **Note requests and answers to prayers in the Prayer Log.**

3. _____ (5 minutes) **End in prayer.**

# Leader's Guide for Chapter 7
# MARKETING

**OVERVIEW OF CHAPTER 7:** The thrust of this chapter is God's demand for us to market and sell with integrity and absolute honesty. Only then is God honored. The leader should read the Marketing Notes prior to attending class.

### AGENDA:

1. _____ (5 minutes) **Open in prayer.**

2. _____ (5 minutes) **Everyone individually recites from memory:**
   *"You shall not steal, nor deal falsely, nor lie to one another"* (Leviticus 19:11).

3. _____ (85 minutes) **Begin the group discussion.**

## DAY ONE – REVIEW CHAPTER 6

**Read the Organization Notes and answer.**

1. What in the Notes was particularly helpful or challenging?

2. How will you apply what you learned to your personal and business life?

## DAY TWO – HONESTY

**Read Leviticus 19:11.** "*You shall not steal, nor deal falsely, nor lie to one another.*"

**And read 1 Peter 1:15-16.** "*Be holy yourselves also in all your behavior; because it is written, 'You shall be holy, for I am holy.'*"

1. What do these verses communicate to you about God's demand for honesty?

   *Leviticus 19:11* — [ **The Lord commands us to be honest.** ]

   *1 Peter 1:15-16* — [ **We are to be holy in our behavior just as the Lord is holy.** ]

**Read Proverbs 26:28.** "*A lying tongue hates those it crushes.*"

**And read Romans 13:9-10.** "*If you love your neighbor as much as you love yourself, you will not want to harm or cheat him, or kill him or steal from him. . . . Love does no wrong to anyone*" (TLB).

2. According to these passages, can you practice dishonesty and still love your neighbor? Why or why not?

   [ **No. Dishonesty always hurts people. However, love does no wrong to a neighbor. We cannot love and be dishonest at the same time.** ]

3. Are you consistently honest in even the smallest details of your business, especially in marketing and sales? If not, what will you do to change?

## DAY THREE — MARKETING

1. Describe the basic marketing and sales practices of your business that have been the most successful.

2. How is integrity in marketing and sales most often compromised in your industry?

3. In what ways are you most tempted to compromise in your marketing and sales?

**Leader** — You should have approximately **one hour** of class time remaining. We recommend a three-minute stretch break for your group at this time.

## DAY FOUR — PRICING AND DISCOUNTS

**Read Deuteronomy 25:13, 15-16.** *"Do not have two differing weights in your bag—one heavy, one light. . . . You must have accurate and honest measures. . . . For the Lord your God detests anyone who does these things, anyone who deals dishonestly"* (NIV).

**And read Proverbs 11:1.** *"A false balance is an abomination to the Lord, but a just weight is His delight."*

1. What do these verses say about pricing your products or services honestly?

   *Deuteronomy 25:13, 15-16*—[ **We must honestly represent what we are selling.** ]

   *Proverbs 11:1*—[ **The Lord hates it when are dishonest in business but delights in our honesty.** ]

2. Describe your pricing and discount policy.

3. Describe any changes in your pricing or discounting that you need to make to please the Lord.

## DAY FIVE — RESTITUTION AND BRIBES

**Read Leviticus 6:4-5.** *"Then it shall be, when he sins and becomes guilty that he shall restore what he took by robbery . . . or anything about which he swore falsely; he shall make restitution for it in full, and add to it one-fifth more. He shall give it to the one to whom it belongs."*

**And read Luke 19:8.** *"If I have defrauded anyone of anything, I will give back four times as much."*

1. What does the Bible say about restitution?

   [ **Restitution was required under Old Testament law. Zaccheus is an example of a person fulfilling this requirement. Restitution involved the return of the item acquired dishonestly plus a penalty.** ]

2. If you have acquired anything dishonestly, how will you make restitution?

**Read Exodus 23:8.** *"Do not accept a bribe, for a bribe blinds those who see and twists the words of the righteous"* (NIV).

**And read Proverbs 15:27.** *"A greedy man brings trouble to his family, but he who hates bribes will live"* (NIV).

3. What does the Bible say about bribes? [ **Never take a bribe; it will influence your judgment and bring danger to you and your family.** ]

4. Have you ever been asked to give or take a bribe? If so, describe what happened.

## DAY SIX – CASE STUDY

**Note:** You may choose to read the Marketing Notes prior to completing Day Six Homework.

### CASE STUDY
For 10 years Michelle Dixon has owned a residential mortgage brokerage that specializes in house loans for those with poor credit ratings. Her office serves a growing community where about 40 percent of the population are relatively recent immigrants to the United States. Their newness to the culture means they are not educated borrowers.

A number of new competitors have entered into the market within the past two years. They market aggressively and do not disclose accurately the interest rate and fees that will be charged.

Michelle's business is off more than 50 percent even though the housing market for her clients is strong. She worries that the business will not survive. She is considering changing her marketing strategy from one of honest disclosure to one that similar to her new competition.

### Analysis
1. Define the problem/issue.

2. Identity the people involved.

3. Identify special circumstances and potential consequences.

4. What actions do you think should be taken? Why?

5. How would God be honored and glorified by these actions?

**Application**
Based on this case study and what you have learned from the Marketing lesson, please answer the following questions.

1. What insight have you gained concerning your business?

2. What changes might you need to make in the operation of your business?

3. What results would you hope to see?

## PRACTICAL APPLICATION

Analyze your existing marketing policies and practices. Describe what changes, if any, you need to make.

### REMAINING AGENDA

1. _____ (10 minutes) **Play the Chapter 7 segment of the *Video*. Answer any questions from the participants.**

    - Read the Marketing Notes on pages 118-125 in the *Manual*.
    - Complete the Planning Homework on pages 128-132 in the *Manual*.
    - Memorize Proverbs 21:5.

2. **Ask your students to be thinking about a "lifetime" or "long-term" prayer request for next week.**

3. _____ (10 minutes) **Note requests and answers to prayers in the Prayer Logs.**

4. _____ (5 minutes) **End in prayer.**

**Reminder:**
Instruct your students to complete the Involvement and Suggestions sheet found in the back of the Manual. Their input is very important for the continued improvement of this study. The completed sheets should be turned in to you and then forwarded to your church leader or to CROWN FINANCIAL MINISTRIES. Students may also complete them by visiting CROWN's Web site at **Crown.org/Business** or by mail at 601 Broad Street, Gainesville, GA 30501.

# Leader's Guide for Chapter 8
# PLANNING

**OVERVIEW OF CHAPTER 8:** Personal planning to grow closer to Christ is key for business leaders because of the influence they have on the entire business. Business planning also is fundamental to the success of a business.

### AGENDA:

1. _____ (5 minutes) **Open in prayer.**

2. _____ (5 minutes) **Each person individually recites from memory:**

   *"The plans of the diligent lead to profit as surely as haste leads to poverty"* (**Proverbs 21:5,** NIV).

3. _____ (85 minutes) **Begin the group discussion.**

## DAY ONE – REVIEW CHAPTER 7 NOTES

**Read the Marketing Notes and answer.**

1. What in the Notes was particularly helpful or challenging?

2. How will you apply what you learned to your personal and business life?

## DAY TWO – PLANNING

**Read Proverbs 21:5.** *"The plans of the diligent lead to profit as surely as haste leads to poverty."*

1. What does this verse say about the benefits of planning and the consequences of not planning?

   **[ Diligent people plan, placing them in a position to prosper. Others rush ahead without a plan and suffer financially. ]**

2. Describe your experience with business planning. What results have you seen?

**Read Luke 14:28-30.** *"For which one of you, when he wants to build a tower, does not first sit down and calculate the cost, to see if he has enough to complete it? Otherwise, when he has laid a foundation and is not able to finish, all who observe it begin to ridicule him, saying, 'This man began to build and was not able to finish.'"*

3. How does the Lord view planning according to this illustration?

   [ **The Lord assumes that wise people will plan to determine if they have sufficient money to start and finish a business or project.** ]

**Read Psalm 20:4.** *"May he [the Lord] give you the desire of your heart and make all your plans succeed"* (NIV).

**And read Proverbs 16:9.** *"Man plans his way, but the Lord directs his steps."*

4. According to these passages, what part does God play in your plans?

   [ **We are to plan, but the Lord controls the ultimate outcome.** ]

## DAY THREE — CHAPTER 8 NOTES

Read the Planning Notes on pages 133-146.

1. Make a brief list of the items from the Notes that were particularly helpful or challenging.

2. How will you apply each of these to your personal and business life?

---

**Leader** — You should have approximately **one hour** of class time remaining. We recommend a three-minute stretch break for your group at this time.

## DAY FOUR — PERSONAL PLAN

Draft a plan to practice the disciplines that will help you develop your character and grow closer to Christ. Share your plan with your group. Here are several suggestions.

1. Avoid a plan that is too ambitious to implement immediately.
2. Select a person to hold you accountable to the plan. Decide how often you will meet.
3. If you are married, discuss the following disciplines with your spouse. It is much easier to practice the disciplines if your spouse encourages you or participates.

**MY SPIRITUAL DISCIPLINES PLAN:**

### 1. Bible Reading and Study

*How often—*

*How much time, when, and where—*

*Select the Bible or Bible study program—*

### 2. Prayer

*How often—*

*How much time, when, and where—*

*List people and things for which to pray—*

### 3. Time alone with God

*How often—*

*How much time—*

*Location—*

### 4. Fellowship with other Christians

*How I can become involved in a local church –*

*Type of small group I will participate in—*

*Location and frequency of group meetings—*

### 5. Reading Christian books

*How often—*

*How much time, when, and where—*

*Books I will read—*

# DAY FIVE – BUSINESS MISSION STATEMENT AND BUSINESS PLAN

A Mission Statement is a very important tool. It helps the organization remain focused and reject opportunities and activities that are not consistent with its mission. It should be clear, concise, and short enough to memorize easily. It answers the question, "Why does this business exist?"

**DEVELOP YOUR MISSION STATEMENT AND SHARE IT WITH YOUR GROUP.**

Follow these steps for developing your Mission Statement:
1. Pray.
2. Answer these:

- The product or service is—

- The product or service is used by—

- The purpose of the business is to—

- God's purpose in the business is met by—

- We are fulfilling God's purpose in our business when—

3. Discuss the answers with your leadership team and draft several Mission Statements.
4. Put the drafts aside for two weeks, then meet with your leadership team to edit and select the Mission Statement.
5. Review after six months and modify as necessary.

**DEVELOP YOUR BUSINESS PLAN.**
(See pages 142-144 for a Business Plan outline.)

**DESCRIBE YOUR PLAN FOR ACCOUNTABILITY TO EXECUTE THE BUSINESS PLAN.**

## DAY SIX – THE ENTIRE STUDY

1. What has been the most helpful part of this entire study for you?

2. Are you going to become part of a continuing small group? If so, describe how you plan to do so.

---

**REMAINING AGENDA**

1. _____ (10 minutes) **Play the Chapter 8 segment of the *Video*. Answer any questions the students may have.**

2. _____ (5 minutes) **Collect the students' Involvement and Suggestions sheets.**

3. _____ (5 minutes) **Take long-term prayer requests and note them in the Prayer Logs.**

4. _____ (5 minutes) **Leaders pray for each student individually.**

**Reminder:** Please forward the Involvement and Suggestions sheets to your church or city leader or to Crown Financial Ministries at 610 Broad Street, Gainesville, GA 30501. You may also transmit the information by visiting Crown's Web site at **Crown.org/Business**.

We suggest that you write each member (or couple) a personal, encouraging letter or e-mail summarizing what you appreciate most about them. May the Lord richly bless you in every way for serving others.

# Leader's Evaluation and Suggestions

Crown wants your counsel. The suggestions and insights of past participants have significantly improved the study. Please fill out both sides of this form. For your convenience, this form may be folded, sealed, and mailed to Crown Financial Ministries, postage paid (see the back of this form). To help save postage and processing costs, you may also complete this form online at **Crown.org/Business**.

**Please Print**

YOUR NAME ☐ MR ☐ MRS ☐ MISS ☐ DR ☐ REV

HOME ADDRESS

CITY    ST/PROV    ZIP/POSTAL CODE

COUNTRY

E-MAIL ADDRESS

HOME PHONE    WORK PHONE

CHURCH NAME

CHURCH ADDRESS

CITY    ST/PROV    ZIP/POSTAL CODE

## NEWSLETTER AND E-MAIL

We send a weekly e-mail message and monthly newsletter sharing God's principles and communicating what the Lord is doing in Crown Financial Ministries. Please indicate below if you would like to receive these.

- ☐ Yes, I would like to receive Crown's weekly e-mail message.
- ☐ Yes, I would like to receive the monthly *Money Matters* newsletter.
- ☐ Yes, I would like to receive the monthly *Money Matters* newsletter by e-mail.

## INVOLVEMENT

**PRAY**

- ☐ Yes, I would like to pray regularly for the Lord to expand Crown and change lives through this ministry.

**SUPPORT**

- ☐ Enclosed is a contribution to Crown in the amount of $_____.
- ☐ I want to become a regular supporter of Crown (a Crown Outreach Partner). Enclosed is my first contribution in the amount of $_____.

75

**BUSINESS REPLY MAIL**
FIRST-CLASS MAIL   PERMIT NO 95   GAINESVILLE GA

POSTAGE WILL BE PAID BY ADDRESSEE

Crown Financial Ministries
PO Box 100
Gainesville GA 30503-9931

*Please tri-fold and seal. Do not staple.*

1. As a leader, please indicate the most significant impact of this study on your **students**:
   - ❑ Prayed to receive Christ # _____
   - ❑ Spiritual intimacy with God increased
   - ❑ Debt reduced
   - ❑ Savings increased
   - ❑ Giving increased
   - ❑ Relationships developed
   - ❑ Accountability increased
   - ❑ Leaders developed # _____
   - ❑ Made decision to participate long-term in a group of other business people

   Additional comments:
   _____
   _____
   _____

2. Please share a brief testimony related to leading this study.
   _____
   _____
   _____
   _____
   _____
   _____

3. Do you have any practical hints that you would suggest to improve the study?
   _____
   _____
   _____

# Student Evaluation

It is important to track the performance of your students to determine who is faithful. Place your students' names where indicated and place an "x" each week in the appropriate box when they have been faithful in their attendance, Scripture memory, or homework. Leave a box blank if they are not faithful in that particular area. Extra copies of this form may be printed from the CD-ROM in the back of this *Leader's Guide*.

| WEEK ENDING | Student Name ➤ REQUIREMENTS | | | | | |
|---|---|---|---|---|---|---|
| 1 | ATTENDANCE | | | | | |
|   | SCRIPTURE MEMORY | | | | | |
|   | HOMEWORK | | | | | |
| 2 | ATTENDANCE | | | | | |
|   | SCRIPTURE MEMORY | | | | | |
|   | HOMEWORK | | | | | |
| 3 | ATTENDANCE | | | | | |
|   | SCRIPTURE MEMORY | | | | | |
|   | HOMEWORK | | | | | |
| 4 | ATTENDANCE | | | | | |
|   | SCRIPTURE MEMORY | | | | | |
|   | HOMEWORK | | | | | |
| 5 | ATTENDANCE | | | | | |
|   | SCRIPTURE MEMORY | | | | | |
|   | HOMEWORK | | | | | |
| 6 | ATTENDANCE | | | | | |
|   | SCRIPTURE MEMORY | | | | | |
|   | HOMEWORK | | | | | |
| 7 | ATTENDANCE | | | | | |
|   | SCRIPTURE MEMORY | | | | | |
|   | HOMEWORK | | | | | |
| 8 | ATTENDANCE | | | | | |
|   | SCRIPTURE MEMORY | | | | | |
|   | HOMEWORK | | | | | |

# CARE LOG

Leaders: _____

Beginning Date of Small Group Study: _____

| WEEK | Initials of leader responsible for contact | Student(s) | Student(s) | Student(s) | Student(s) | Student(s) | Student(s) |
|---|---|---|---|---|---|---|---|
| 1 | | | | | | | |
| 2 | | | | | | | |
| 3 | | | | | | | |
| 4 | | | | | | | |
| 5 | | | | | | | |
| 6 | | | | | | | |
| 7 | | | | | | | |
| 8 | | | | | | | |

Description of first social activity (conduct about week 4):




Description of second social activity (conduct about week 8):

# PRAYER LOGS
## Be Faithful in Prayer

"Pray for one another.... The effective prayer
of a righteous man can accomplish much"
(James 5:16).

# "Pray for one another" (JAMES 5:16).

Name _____  Spouse _____
Home phone _____  Children (ages) _____
Business phone _____  _____
Cell phone _____  _____
E-mail _____  _____
Home address _____  _____
_____   _____

| WEEK | PRAYER REQUEST(S) | ANSWERS TO PRAYER |
|---|---|---|
| 1 | | |
| 2 | | |
| 3 | | |
| 4 | | |
| 5 | | |
| 6 | | |
| 7 | | |
| 8 | My long-term prayer request: | |

PRAYER LOG

# "Pray for one another" (James 5:16).

Name _____  Spouse _____
Home phone _____  Children (ages) _____
Business phone _____  _____
Cell phone _____  _____
E-mail _____  _____
Home address _____  _____
_____

| Week | Prayer Request(s) | Answers to Prayer |
|---|---|---|
| 1 | | |
| 2 | | |
| 3 | | |
| 4 | | |
| 5 | | |
| 6 | | |
| 7 | | |
| 8 | My long-term prayer request: | |

PRAYER LOG

# "Pray for one another" (JAMES 5:16).

Name _____  Spouse _____
Home phone _____  Children (ages) _____
Business phone _____  _____
Cell phone _____  _____
E-mail _____  _____
Home address _____  _____
_____  _____

| Week | Prayer Request(s) | Answers to Prayer |
|---|---|---|
| 1 | | |
| 2 | | |
| 3 | | |
| 4 | | |
| 5 | | |
| 6 | | |
| 7 | | |
| 8 | My long-term prayer request: | |

PRAYER LOG

82

# "Pray for one another" (James 5:16).

Name _____  Spouse _____
Home phone _____  Children (ages) _____
Business phone _____  _____
Cell phone _____  _____
E-mail _____  _____
Home address _____  _____
_____   _____

| Week | Prayer Request(s) | Answers to Prayer |
|---|---|---|
| 1 | | |
| 2 | | |
| 3 | | |
| 4 | | |
| 5 | | |
| 6 | | |
| 7 | | |
| 8 | My long-term prayer request: | |

PRAYER LOG

# "Pray for one another" (James 5:16).

Name _____  Spouse _____
Home phone _____  Children (ages) _____
Business phone _____  _____
Cell phone _____  _____
E-mail _____  _____
Home address _____  _____
_____  _____

| Week | Prayer Request(s) | Answers to Prayer |
|---|---|---|
| 1 | | |
| 2 | | |
| 3 | | |
| 4 | | |
| 5 | | |
| 6 | | |
| 7 | | |
| 8 | My long-term prayer request: | |

PRAYER LOG

# "Pray for one another" (James 5:16).

Name _____  Spouse _____
Home phone _____  Children (ages) _____
Business phone _____  _____
Cell phone _____  _____
E-mail _____  _____
Home address _____  _____
_____  _____

| Week | Prayer Request(s) | Answers to Prayer |
|---|---|---|
| 1 | | |
| 2 | | |
| 3 | | |
| 4 | | |
| 5 | | |
| 6 | | |
| 7 | | |
| 8 | My long-term prayer request: | |

PRAYER LOG

# "Pray for one another" (James 5:16).

Name _____  Spouse _____
Home phone _____  Children (ages) _____
Business phone _____  _____
Cell phone _____  _____
E-mail _____  _____
Home address _____  _____
_____  _____

| Week | Prayer Request(s) | Answers to Prayer |
|---|---|---|
| 1 | | |
| 2 | | |
| 3 | | |
| 4 | | |
| 5 | | |
| 6 | | |
| 7 | | |
| 8 | My long-term prayer request: | |

PRAYER LOG

86

# "Pray for one another" (JAMES 5:16).

Name _____  Spouse _____
Home phone _____  Children (ages) _____
Business phone _____  _____
Cell phone _____  _____
E-mail _____  _____
Home address _____  _____
_____  _____

| WEEK | PRAYER REQUEST(S) | ANSWERS TO PRAYER |
|---|---|---|
| 1 | | |
| 2 | | |
| 3 | | |
| 4 | | |
| 5 | | |
| 6 | | |
| 7 | | |
| 8 | My long-term prayer request: | |

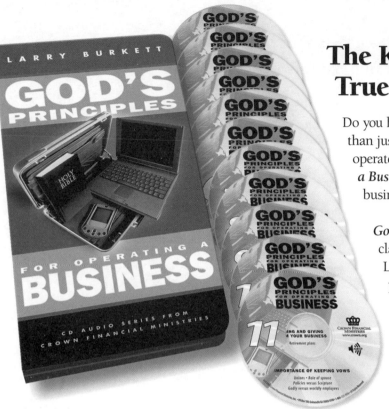

# The Key to Understanding True Business Success

Do you have the desire to do more in the marketplace than just make money? Ever wonder how God would operate a business? *God's Principles for Operating a Business* will help point the way to achieving business success God's way.

*God's Principles for Operating a Business*, a classic seminar taught by author and teacher Larry Burkett (1939-2003), presents 36 principles on 11 CDs (over 8 hours of teaching!) that will set any business apart from the rest.

Operating a business according to God's Word will produce a new level of success in ways you never thought possible!

**Topics in this series –**

1. History of Business in America / What the future may hold
2. How to treat suppliers, employees, customers and owners / Danger of business bondage
3. Fundamentals of business planning / Discipline and delegation
4. Principles that ensure a balanced lifestyle / Short-term goals
5. Employing the unemployable / Jobs for young people / Retirement and inheritance
6. Steps to dismissal / Paying a fair wage / Selecting Managers
7. Borrowing / Lending / Collecting Debts
8. How to handle lawsuits / Corporations / Partnerships
9. Danger of compromise
10. Tithing and giving from your business / Retirement plans
11. Importance of keeping vows / Unions / Role of spouse / Policies versus Scripture / Godly versus worldly employees

*God's Principles for Operating a Business*
ISBN# 1-56427-099-8

• • • • • • • • • • • • • • • • • • • • • • • • •

# Read the book that is the foundation for this small group study!

*Business by the Book* offers radical principles of business management that go beyond the Ten Commandments and other biblical maxims. It gives a step-by-step presentation of how businesses should be run according to the Creator of all management rules. Find out what God's Word says on topics such as:

✓ Hiring and firing decisions
✓ Pay increases and promotions
✓ Management selection
✓ Employee pay decisions
✓ Borrowing and/or lending decisions
✓ Discounting policies
✓ Forming corporations and partnerships
✓ Business tithing requirements

*Business by the Book*
ISBN# 0-7852-7141-4
(294 Pages, soft cover)

To order, contact your local bookstore or contact Crown at Crown.org or 1-800-722-1976.